A Humans Guide To:

DRINKING WITH DOGS

By N.K

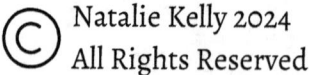 Natalie Kelly 2024
All Rights Reserved

Table of Contents

1 - Security Checkpoint

3 - Introduction

4 - Benefits of drinking with your dog

5 - Safety Considerations

7 - Ingredients to avoid

8 - Be a responsible pet parent

10 - Serving sizes

11 - Dog friendly events

12 - Smaller events

13 - Larger events

14 - At the pub

15 - Weddings

19 - Social Etiquette

22 - The Do's & Don'ts

23 - Dog friendly hosting: Tips & tricks

26 - Event checklist

27 - Doggy drink recipes

43 - Doggy treats & snack recipes

60 - Thank you note

This book is intended for humans of legal drinking age only.

All activities, including dog friendly recipes, in this book require adult supervision at all times.

Introduction

Welcome dog parents & friends!
Drinking with your dog can be a pawsitively fun experience!
Imagine a sunny afternoon, a refreshing drink in hand, and your loyal companion by your side.
There's something undeniably special about sharing these moments with your furry friend, and incorporating them into your social gatherings can add a whole new level of joy and camaraderie.
This book is your guide to creating safe, fun & unforgettable experiences that combine your love of dogs with your enjoyment of responsible drinking culture.
Whether you're hosting a backyard party, attending a dog-friendly event, at the local pub or simply relaxing at home, there are countless ways to safely include your dog in your adventures.
We've even included dog friendly recipes for drinks & snacks to ensure your furry friend has a tail wagging good time no matter the occasion!

Always remember to drink in moderation, be a responsible pet owner & consider your dog's individual circumstances.

Benefits of Drinking with Your Dog

* Strengthened bond: Spending quality time with your dog can deepen your connection and strengthen your bond.

* Increased happiness: Dogs have a remarkable ability to brighten our moods and reduce stress.

* Socialization opportunities: Dog-friendly events provide opportunities to meet new people and socialize with other dog owners.

* Shared experiences: Creating shared memories with your dog can enrich your life and bring you closer together.

Remember: While this book offers tips and suggestions for enjoying your time with your dog, it's essential to prioritize your pet's well-being. Always ensure that your dog is safe and comfortable, and avoid activities that could put them at risk

.

Get ready to embark on a fun-filled journey with your furry companion. Let's raise a glass to good times, great company, and the unconditional love of our canine companions!

SAFETY CONSIDERATIONS

Safety Considerations

Alcohol is highly toxic to dogs and can have serious health consequences, even in small amounts. The effects of alcohol poisoning in dogs can include:

 * Vomiting
 * Diarrhea
 * Lethargy
 * Difficulty walking or coordinating movements
 * Loss of consciousness
 * Respiratory failure

If you suspect that your dog has ingested alcohol, it is important to seek veterinary attention immediately. Do not wait for symptoms to worsen. To prevent your dog from accidentally consuming alcohol, follow these safety tips:

 * Secure alcoholic beverages: Keep all alcoholic drinks out of reach of your dog, including open containers and spilled drinks.
 * Be mindful of discarded items: Dispose of empty cans, bottles, and glasses promptly.
 * Avoid leaving alcohol unattended: Never leave alcoholic beverages unattended, even for a short time.
 * Educate others: Inform guests and family members about the dangers of alcohol for dogs and request their cooperation in keeping your pet safe

Food & Drink Ingredients To Avoid

This list contains common food & drink ingredients that can be toxic to dogs

* Avocado
* Grapes
* Raisins
" Rhubarb
* Mushrooms
* Onions
* Chives
* Leeks
* Shallots
* Garlic
* Tomato stems
* Unripe/green tomatoes
* Chocolate
* Xylitol
* Macadamia nuts
* Almonds (unroasted or raw)
* Pistachios (unroasted or raw)
* All Alcohol
* Coffee
* Black tea
* Raw yeast dough
" Dry yeast
* Moldy food
* Sago palm seeds
* Castor beans
* Sugar

It's important to note that even small amounts of these substances can be toxic to dogs. If you suspect your dog has ingested any of these substances, seek veterinary attention immediately.

Be a responsible pet parent

it's crucial to prioritize your dog's safety and well-being, especially when alcohol is involved. Here are some essential tips to keep in mind:

1. Never let your dog consume alcohol: Alcohol is highly toxic to dogs and can cause severe health problems, even in small amounts. The effects of alcohol poisoning in dogs can include vomiting, diarrhea, lethargy, difficulty walking, loss of consciousness, and respiratory failure. If you suspect your dog has ingested alcohol, seek veterinary attention immediately.
2. Secure alcoholic beverages: Store all alcoholic drinks out of your dog's reach. This includes open containers, spilled drinks, and discarded cans or bottles.
3. Be mindful of discarded items: Dispose of empty cans, bottles, and glasses promptly to prevent your dog from accidentally ingesting them.
4. Avoid leaving alcohol unattended: Never leave alcoholic beverages unattended, even for a short time. Your dog may be tempted to investigate and potentially consume the drink.

5. Educate others: Inform guests and family members about the dangers of alcohol for dogs and request their cooperation in keeping your pet safe.

6. Monitor your dog's behavior: Pay attention to your dog's behavior when around alcohol. If you notice any signs of intoxication, such as vomiting, lethargy, or difficulty walking, seek veterinary attention immediately.

7. Limit alcohol consumption in your dog's presence: While it's not necessary to avoid alcohol consumption entirely, it's important to be mindful of your dog's presence. If you're drinking heavily, consider leaving your dog with a trusted friend or family member.

8. Provide alternative activities: Keep your dog entertained with toys, treats, and games tol. Offer dog safe drinks & treats from our recipe list!

9. Be a responsible host: If you're hosting a party with alcohol, ensure there is a designated area for dogs to play and socialize away from the festivities.

10. Set a good example: Your dog learns from your behavior. By demonstrating responsible alcohol consumption, you're teaching your dog the importance of moderation and safety.

By following these tips, you can help ensure your dog's safety and well-being.

Remember, your dog's health is your top priority.

Serving sizes

Treats should be given as a reward or supplement to their regular diet, not as a primary food source.

To determine the appropriate serving size, consider the following factors:

 * Your dog's size and weight: Larger dogs will require larger portions than smaller dogs.
 * Your dog's activity level: More active dogs may need additional calories.
 * The treat's calorie content: the number of calories per treat.
 * Your dog's overall diet: Ensure treats don't make up a significant portion of your dog's daily caloric intake.

A general guideline is to limit treats to no more than 10% of your dog's daily calorie intake.

If you're unsure about the appropriate serving size, consult with your veterinarian for personalized advice.

DOG FRIENDLY EVENTS

Smaller Events

Backyard Barbecues and Parties:
Hosting a backyard barbecue or party is a great way to spend time with friends and family while enjoying the company of your furry companion. Here are some tips for making your event dog-friendly:

 * Choose a dog-friendly venue: If you're planning a party at a friend's house, make sure their property is fenced and safe for dogs.
 * Provide plenty of shade and water: Ensure there are plenty of shaded areas for dogs to rest and plenty of fresh water available.
 * Keep human food and drinks out of reach: Place food and drinks on tables or elevated surfaces to prevent dogs from accessing them.
 * Consider a separate dog area: If you have a large number of dogs attending, consider setting up a separate area for them to play and socialize.
 * Provide dog-friendly activities: Keep dogs entertained with toys, treats, and games.
* Ensure all guests are aware of the dog on site & that all entry gates/doors are secure at all times.
* Children should be fully supervised with dogs

Larger Events

Festivals, Fairs, and Community Events:
Many communities host dog-fiendly events. These events can be a great way to socialize your dog and have fun. Here are some tips for attending these events:

* Check the event policies: Before attending an event, check the event website or contact the organizers to determine if dogs are allowed.
* Leash laws and waste management: Make sure you comply with all leash laws and waste management regulations.
* Up to date I.D tags in case your pooch gets separated from you.
* Be mindful of other attendees: Be respectful of other attendees, especially those who may be afraid of dogs.
* Avoid crowds & loud noise: If your dog becomes overwhelmed by crowds or noise, find a quieter area for them to rest.
* Stay hydrated: Ensure your dog has plenty of water to drink, especially on hot days.
* Take doggy snacks for long days out.
* A toy and blanket for events when you will be sitting down ie on grass etc.

At The Pub

Taking your dog to the local pub can be a fun and enjoyable experience for both you and your furry friend. However, it's important to prioritize your dog's safety and well-being.

* Always ensure your dog is on a leash and well-behaved.
* Toilet your dog outside of the establishment grounds or in a designated area only & clean up after them.
* Avoid letting your dog jump on people or bark excessively, as this can be disruptive to other patrons.
* Choose a pub with outdoor seating or a designated dog-friendly area.
* Ensure your dog has access to plenty of fresh water and shade, especially on hot days.
* Monitor your dog's behavior and be prepared to leave if they become uncomfortable or agitated.
* Take toys or a chew treat to keep them entertained.
* If your having a meal, take food for your dog.

By following these tips, you can enjoy a safe and enjoyable outing with your furry companion.

Weddings

Attending a wedding with your furry friend can be a wonderful experience. Here are some tips for being a responsible and respectful guest:

1. Check with the Couple: Before bringing your dog to the wedding, always check with the couple to see if it's allowed. Some venues or wedding styles may not be suitable for pets.
2. Consider the Venue: If dogs are allowed, make sure the venue is dog-friendly and can accommodate your pet comfortably. Outdoor weddings are often more suitable for dogs than indoor events.
3. Respect the Other Guests: Not everyone may be comfortable around dogs. Be mindful of others and their comfort levels. Avoid letting your dog jump on people or bark excessively.
4. Keep Your Dog on a Leash: Ensure your dog is always on a leash, even if the venue allows dogs off-leash. This helps to keep your pet safe and under control.
5. Avoid Disruptions: Try to avoid any disruptions that might interfere with the wedding ceremony or reception. This includes keeping your dog quiet and out of the way during important moments.

6. Clean Up After Your Dog: Always pick up after your dog, even if the venue has designated areas for pet waste.
7. Bring Necessary Supplies: Make sure you have everything your dog needs for the day, including food, water, treats, and any necessary medications.
8. Respect the Couple's Wishes: If the couple has specific requests or guidelines for bringing your dog, be sure to follow them.

By following these tips, you can help ensure that your dog's presence at the wedding is a positive one. Remember to be respectful, considerate, and responsible, and enjoy the special occasion with your furry friend by your side.

Your dog friendly wedding

Planning a wedding can be stressful, but adding a furry friend to the mix can make it even more memorable and special. A dog-friendly wedding offers a unique and heartwarming experience for both humans and pets. If you're considering including your dog in your big day, here are some tips to help you plan a successful and enjoyable event.

First and foremost, it's essential to check with your venue to ensure they allow dogs. Some venues may have specific policies or restrictions regarding pets, so it's important to clarify these details upfront. Once you have the venue's approval, you can start planning the rest of your dog-friendly wedding.

Once you have the venue's approval, here are some additional considerations to keep in mind when planning your dog-friendly wedding:

 * Guest List: Consider how many guests will be bringing their dogs. This will help you determine the appropriate size of the venue and any necessary accommodations.

 * Wedding Style: A casual outdoor wedding is often the best choice for a dog-friendly event. However, even indoor venues can accommodate dogs if they have appropriate outdoor spaces.

 * Dog-Friendly Activities: Plan some dog-friendly activities or games to keep your guests' furry friends entertained. This could include a dog-themed scavenger hunt, a pet photo booth, or a designated play area.

* Dog Wedding Attire: While it's not mandatory for dogs to wear special attire at a wedding, dressing your furry friend up in a festive outfit can be a fun way to include them in the celebration. Consider their personality and comfort level when choosing an outfit. A simple bandana or bow tie can be a stylish and comfortable option. If your dog is more adventurous, you might choose a themed costume or a matching outfit for you and your pet. Remember, the most important thing is that your dog feels comfortable and happy in their attire.

* Dog-Friendly Vendors: When choosing vendors for your wedding, look for those who are dog-friendly and have experience working with pets. This could include caterers, photographers, and musicians.

* Emergency Contact Information: Provide your guests with the contact information for a local veterinarian in case of any emergencies.

By carefully considering these factors, you can plan a memorable and enjoyable dog-friendly wedding that everyone will love. Remember, the most important thing is to ensure the safety and comfort of both your human and canine guests.

SOCIAL ETIQUETTE

Social Etiquette

Being a Responsible Pet Owner in Public

As a dog owner, it's essential to be mindful of others and their comfort levels when you're out and about with your furry friend. Here are some tips for practicing good doggie etiquette in public places:

Around Other People

 * Leash Laws: Always adhere to local leash laws. Even if your dog is well-behaved, it's important to keep them on a leash in public areas.

 * Avoid Excessive Barking: If your dog barks excessively, try to calm them down or find a quieter area. Excessive barking can be disruptive to others.

 * Respect Personal Space: Ask permission before allowing your dog to approach or interact with other people. Not everyone may be comfortable with dogs.

 * Clean Up After Your Dog: Always pick up after your dog. This is a basic courtesy and helps to keep public spaces clean and safe.

Around Children

* Teach Your Dog to Be Gentle: Train your dog to be gentle around children, especially young children.
* Supervise Interactions: Always supervise interactions between your dog and children.
* Educate Children: Teach children how to interact with dogs safely and respectfully.

Around Other Dogs

* Leash Laws: Ensure both your dog and other dogs are on leashes.
* Avoid Aggressive Behavior: If your dog exhibits aggressive behavior, consult with a professional trainer.
* Respect Other Dogs' Space: Allow dogs to approach each other at their own pace.
* Prevent Dog Fights: If you see a potential dog fight, intervene calmly and safely.

Remember, being a responsible pet owner means respecting others and their comfort levels. By following these guidelines, you can help create a positive and enjoyable experience for everyone.

The Do's & Don'ts

5 Do's for Dog Social Etiquette:
 * Ask before approaching: Always ask the owner's permission before allowing your dog to greet theirs.
 * Leash up: Keep your dog on a leash in public areas, unless specifically allowed.
 * Clean up after your dog: Responsible pet ownership includes picking up after your dog.
 * Respect personal space: Not everyone is comfortable with dogs. Give people space if they seem hesitant.
 * Be mindful of noise: Excessive barking can be disruptive. Try to keep your dog calm and quiet.

5 Don'ts for Dog Social Etiquette:
 * Don't let your dog jump on people. This can be seen as rude and even aggressive.
 * Don't allow your dog to approach other dogs without permission. This can lead to unwanted interactions or even fights.
 * Don't let your dog beg for food. This can encourage bad behavior and create tension.
 * Don't leave your dog unattended. Always supervise your dog in public areas.
 * Don't ignore your dog's body language. If your dog seems anxious or stressed, give them space.

Dog Friendly Hosting: Tip & Tricks

Hosting dog friendly events

Tips for Dog-Friendly Events

When hosting a dog-friendly event, it's essential to prioritize the safety and well-being of both your human and canine guests. Here are some tips for responsible hosting:

1. Set Clear Expectations: Communicate your expectations for dog behavior to your guests beforehand. This includes leash laws, waste management, and any specific rules or restrictions.
2. Provide a Safe Environment: Ensure your venue is secure and free of hazards that could harm dogs. This includes fencing, poisonous plants, and any potential choking hazards.
3. Offer Plenty of Water and Shade: Provide ample fresh water and shaded areas for dogs to rest and cool down, especially during hot weather.
4. Consider Dietary Needs: If you're providing food, be mindful of dietary restrictions or allergies among your guests' dogs. Offer a variety of dog-friendly treats and snacks.

5. Manage Waste: Provide plenty of waste bags and designated areas for pet waste disposal.
6. Supervise Interactions: Keep an eye on interactions between dogs and humans to ensure everyone's safety and comfort.
7. Plan for Emergencies: Have a plan in place in case of any accidents or emergencies. This includes knowing the location of the nearest veterinarian and having emergency contact information on hand.
8. Respect Noise Levels: Be mindful of noise levels, especially if there are neighbors or other nearby residents. Loud noise can be distressing for dogs and may lead to complaints.
9. Clean Up After the Event: Thoroughly clean up the venue after the event to remove any debris or hazards that could harm dogs.
10. Send Thank-You Notes: Show your appreciation to your guests for attending your dog-friendly event. A personalized thank-you note can go a long way in fostering positive relationships.

By following these guidelines, you can ensure that your dog-friendly event is a safe, enjoyable, and memorable experience for everyone involved.

Event Checklist

Pre-Event Planning:
 * Venue selection
 * Guest list
 * Budget
 * Activities
 * Food and drinks menu
 * Order supplies
 * Vendor selection
 * Marketing and promotion
 * Emergency preparedness

Day-of Event:
 * Set up
 * Welcome guests
 * Manage activities
 * Photos/ videos
 * Food and drinks
 * Clean-up
 * Thank guests
 * Party bags

Post-Event:
 * Feedback
 * Thank vendors
 * Follow up

Doggy Drink Recipes

IMPORTANT NOTE

Ensure your dog has access to fresh water at all times.

These recipes are designed as a treat.

They should be given in small quantities, in moderation & as part of a healthy diet.

Substituting Ingredients

If your dog has allergies or does not find certain ingredients palatable, get creative & substitute ingredients with another dog friendly item from our recipes.

Have fun with it! Mix & match ingredients to create your pups own unique cocktail or treat!

 # Bark-arita Margaritas

Ingredients:
* 1/4 cup spinach juice
* 1/4 cup coconut water
* 1 tablespoon honey
* Lime slice to garnish

Equipment:
* Blender or shaker
* Measuring cups and spoons
* Serving bowl or plastic cocktail glass

Instructions:
* Gather your ingredients: Place the spinach juice, coconut water, and honey in a blender.
* Blend until smooth: Blend the ingredients on high speed until the mixture is smooth and combined.
* Serve: Pour the Bark-arita into a serving bowl or directly into your dog's bowl.
* Enjoy: Your dog will love the tangy and refreshing flavors of this healthy treat.

Tips:
* For a sweeter Bark-arita, add more honey.
* For a less sweet option, omit the honey altogether.
* You can store leftover Bark-arita in the refrigerator for up to a week.

Strawberry Dog-quiri

Ingredients:
* 1 cup fresh strawberries chopped
* 1/2 cup plain yogurt
* 1/4 cup coconut water
* 1 tablespoon honey (optional)

Equipment:
* Blender or shaker
* Measuring cups
* Serving bowl or plastic cocktail glass

Instructions:
* Combine ingredients: Place the strawberries, yogurt, coconut water, and honey (if using) in a blender.
* Blend until smooth: Blend the ingredients on high speed until the mixture is smooth and creamy.
* Serve: Pour the Strawberry Daiquiri into a plastic serving glass or directly into your dog's bowl. Granish with strawberry slices

Pupper Pale Ale

Ingredients:
* 1/4 cup potato puree
* 1/4 cup bone broth
* 1/4 cup water
* 1 teaspoon apple cider

Equipment:
* Blender or shaker
* Measuring cups and spoons
* Serving bowl or plastic beer cup

Instructions:
* Gather your ingredients: Place the potato puree, bone broth, water and apple cider in a blender.
* Blend until smooth: Blend the ingredients on high speed until the mixture is smooth and combined.
* Serve: Pour the Pupper Pale Ale into a plastic serving glass or directly into your dog's bowl.
* Enjoy: Your dog will love the hearty and comforting flavors of this healthy treat.

Tips:
* For a thicker consistency, add more potato puree or bone broth.
* You can store leftover Pale Ale in the refrigerator for up to a week.

Mojito Mayhem

Ingredients:
* 1/4 cup cucumber puree
* 1/4 cup green tea
* 3-4 mint leaves chopped

Equipment:
* Blender or shaker
* Measuring cups
* Serving bowl or plastic cocktail glass

Instructions:
* Gather your ingredients: Place the cucumber puree, green tea, and chopped mint leaves in a blender.
* Blend until smooth: Blend the ingredients on high speed until the mixture is smooth and combined.
* Serve: Pour the Mojito Mayhem into a serving bowl or directly into your dog's bowl.
* Enjoy: Your dog will love the green and refreshing flavors of this healthy treat.

Tip:
* You can store leftover Mojito Mayhem in the refrigerator for up to a week.

Puppy Love On The Beach

Ingredients:
* 1/4 cup mango puree
* 1/4 cup pineapple juice
* 1/4 cup coconut milk

Equipment:
* Blender
* Measuring cups and spoons
* Serving bowl or plastic cup

Instructions:
* Gather your ingredients: Place the mango puree, pineapple juice, and coconut milk in a blender.
* Blend until smooth: Blend the ingredients on high speed until the mixture is smooth and combined.
* Serve: Pour the Margarita Madness into a serving bowl or directly into your dog's bowl.
* Enjoy: Your dog will love the tropical flavors of this healthy treat.

Tips:
* For a sweeter Margarita Madness, add a touch of honey or maple syrup.
* You can store leftover Margarita Madness in the refrigerator for up to a week.

Rovers Red Wine

Ingredients:
* 1/4 cup cranberry juice
* 1/4 cup bone broth
* 1 tablespoon honey

Equipment:
* Blender or shaker
* Measuring cups
* Serving bowl or plastic wine glass

Instructions:
* Gather your ingredients: Place the cranberry juice, bone broth, and honey in a blender.
* Blend until smooth: Blend the ingredients on high speed until the mixture is smooth and combined.
* Serve: Pour the wine into a plastic wine glass or directly into your dog's bowl.

Tips:
* For a thicker consistency, add more cranberry juice or bone broth.
* You can store leftover wine in the refrigerator for up to a week.

Howloween Brew

Ingredients:
* 1/4 cup pumpkin puree
* 1/4 cup bone broth
* 1/4 cup coconut milk

Equipment:
* Blender or shaker
* Measuring cups
* Serving bowl or plastic cocktail glass

Instructions:
* Gather your ingredients: Place the pumpkin puree, bone broth, and coconut milk in a blender.
* Blend until smooth: Blend the ingredients on high speed until the mixture is smooth and combined.
* Serve: Pour the beer into a serving bowl or directly into your dog's bowl.
* Enjoy: Your dog will love the sweet and comforting flavors of this healthy treat.

Tips:
* For a thicker consistency, add more pumpkin puree or bone broth.
* You can store leftover beer in the refrigerator for up to 2 days

Pawsecco

Ingredients:
* 1/4 cup coconut water
* 1/4 cup chicken broth
* 1/4 cup pure sparkling water

Equipment:
* Shaker
* Measuring cups
* Serving bowl or plastic cup

Instructions:
* Gather your ingredients: Place the coconut water, chicken broth & sparkling water in a cocktail shaker.
* Shake until the mixture is smooth and combined.
* Serve: Pour the Pawsecco into a plastic cup or directly into your dog's bowl.

Tips:
* For a sweeter Pawsecco, add a touch of honey or maple syrup.
* You can store leftover Pawsecco in the refrigerator for up to a week.
* Use pure sparkling water with no additives such as sugar, flavours or xylitol.

Doggy Eggnog

Ingredients:
* 1/4 cup pumpkin puree
* 1/4 cup plain yogurt
1/4 cup coconut milk
* 1/4 teaspoon nutmeg
* 1/4 teaspoon cinnamon

Equipment:
* Blender or shaker
* Measuring cups and spoons
* Serving bowl or plastic drinking glass

Instructions:
* Gather your ingredients: Place the pumpkin puree, coconut milk, plain yogurt, nutmeg, and cinnamon in a blender.
* Blend until smooth: Blend the ingredients on high speed until the mixture is smooth and combined.
* Serve: Pour the eggnog into a festive bowl, plastic glass or directly into your dog's bowl.

Tips:
* For a sweeter eggnog, add a touch of honey or maple syrup.

Canine Cider

Ingredients:
* 1/4 cup coconut water
* 1/4 cup bone broth
* 1 teaspoon apple cider vinegar

Equipment:
* Blender or shaker
* Measuring cups
* Serving bowl or plastic beer cup

Instructions:
* Gather your ingredients: Place the coconut water, bone broth, and apple cider vinegar in a blender.
* Blend until smooth: Blend the ingredients on high speed until the mixture is smooth and combined.
* Serve: Pour the Infusion into a serving bowl or directly into your dog's bowl.
* Enjoy: Your dog will love the savory and nutritious flavors of this healthy treat.

Tips:
* For a stronger flavor, add more bone broth or apple cider vinegar.
* You can store leftover Cider Infusion in the refrigerator for up to a week.

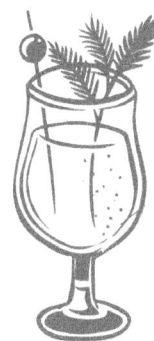 

Gin & Tonic Tails

Ingredients:
* 1/4 cup of chamomile tea
* 1/4 cup cucumber juice
* 1/4 cup bone broth
* 1 tablespoon apple cider vinegar

Equipment:
* Blender or shaker
* Measuring cups and spoons
* Serving bowl or plastic cocktail glass

Instructions:
* Gather your ingredients: Place the chamomile tea, cucumber juice, bone broth, and apple cider vinegar in a blender.
* Blend until smooth: Blend the ingredients on high speed until the mixture is smooth and combined.
* Serve: Pour the Gin and Tonic Tails into a serving bowl or directly into your dog's bowl.
* Enjoy: Your dog will love the savory and hydrating flavors of this healthy treat.

Tip:
* You can store leftover Gin and Tonic Tails in the refrigerator for up to a week.

Mad Dog Milkshakes

Ingredients:
* 1 cup milk or a milk alternative (almond milk, coconut milk, soy milk)
* 1/2 cup mashed fruit (banana, strawberry, mango, blueberry, or a combination)
* 1/4 cup plain yogurt
* 1 tablespoon honey (optional)

Instructions:
* Combine ingredients: Place the milk or milk alternative, mashed fruit, yogurt, and honey (if desired) in a blender or shaker.
* Blend until smooth: Blend the ingredients on high speed until the mixture is smooth and slushy.
* Serve: Pour the milkshake into a plastic serving glass or bowl.

Tip:
* Experiment with different fruit flavors and milk alternatives to find your dog's favorite combination.

Canine Champagne

Ingredients:
* 1/2 cup sparkling water
* 1/4 cup apple juice
* 1 tablespoon honey

Instructions:
* Combine ingredients: Place the sparkling water, apple juice, and honey in a glass.
* Stir: Stir the ingredients together until the honey is dissolved.
* Serve: Serve the Canine Champagne to your dog in a plastic champagne glass or bowl.

Tips:
* You can adjust the amount of honey and apple juice to your dog's preference.
* Store leftover Canine Champagne in the refrigerator for up to a week.
* Use pure sparkling water without additives like flavours, sugar or xylitol.

Time for Tea!

Did you know that some teas can be a pawsitively healthy treat!? Serve at room temperature or slightly chilled on a hot day & slightly warm on a cold day. Only use organic high quality tea to ensure it is free from chemicals & pesticides.

NOTE: Black tea including variations contain caffeine which is toxic to dogs & should be avoided.aling with all items & ingredients that contain caffeine.

List of Dog Friendly Teas

* Chamomile tea: Known for its calming properties, chamomile tea can help soothe your dog's digestive system and promote relaxation.
* Ginger tea: Ginger is a natural anti-inflammatory and can aid in digestion. It can also help alleviate nausea and vomiting in dogs.
* Peppermint tea: Peppermint is often used to relieve digestive issues such as gas and bloating. It can also help freshen your dog's breath.
* Fennel tea: Fennel is a natural digestive aid that can help reduce flatulence and bloating.
* Licorice root tea: Licorice root has anti-inflammatory properties and can help soothe the digestive tract.
* Lavender tea: Lavender is known for its calming and relaxing properties, making it a great choice for dogs experiencing anxiety or stress.
* Valerian root tea: Valerian root is a natural sedative that can help dogs with anxiety and insomnia.
* Passionflower tea: Passionflower is another herb with calming properties that can be beneficial for anxious dogs.
* Green tea: Green tea contains antioxidants that can support overall health and well-being. However, it's important to offer green tea in moderation as it contains low traces of caffeine

DOGGY TREAT & SNACK RECIPES

Using Alternative Ingredients

When creating dog recipes, it's essential to consider your dog's specific needs and preferences. Some dogs may have allergies or sensitivities to certain ingredients, while others may simply be picky eaters. By understanding common ingredient substitutions and tailoring recipes to your dog's individual tastes, you can ensure they enjoy their meals while staying healthy.

Common Ingredient Allergies and Substitutions

 * Dairy: Dogs with lactose intolerance can benefit from dairy-free alternatives like coconut milk, almond milk, or goat's milk.
 * Gluten: For dogs with gluten sensitivities, substitute wheat flour with alternatives like rice flour, oat flour, or coconut flour.
 * Eggs: Dogs with egg allergies can have their protein needs met with alternatives like lentils, chickpeas, or tofu.
 * Beef: Dogs with beef allergies can enjoy protein-rich alternatives like chicken, turkey, lamb, or fish.

Tips for Adapting Recipes

* Research ingredient substitutions: Before making changes to a recipe, research suitable alternatives to ensure they are safe and nutritious for your dog.
 * Consider your dog's preferences: Observe your dog's eating habits to determine which flavors and textures they enjoy.
 * Experiment gradually: Introduce new ingredients slowly to monitor your dog's reaction and identify any potential sensitivities.
 * Consult with your veterinarian: If you have concerns about your dog's allergies or dietary needs, consult with your veterinarian for personalized advice.

Alternative Ingredient Ideas

* Protein sources: Chicken, turkey, lamb, fish, lentils, chickpeas, tofu, and tempeh.
 * Carbohydrates: Rice, oats, quinoa, sweet potatoes, and brown rice.
 * Fruits and vegetables: Apples, bananas, carrots, spinach, and pumpkin.
 * Dairy alternatives: Coconut milk, almond milk, goat's milk, and plain yogurt..

Remember, the key is to experiment and find what works best for your furry friend.

Margarita Munchies

Ingredients:
* 1 large sweet potato, mashed
* 1/4 cup whole wheat flour
* 1/4 cup rolled oats
* 1 tablespoon lime zest

Equipment:
* Mixing bowl
* Measuring cups and spoons
* Baking sheet * Parchment paper * Rolling pin

Instructions:
* Prepare the ingredients: In a mixing bowl, combine the mashed sweet potato, whole wheat flour, rolled oats, and lime zest.
* Mix well: Use a spatula or your hands to thoroughly combine the ingredients until a dough forms.
* Roll into balls: Divide the dough into bite-sized pieces and roll them into balls using your hands or a rolling pin.
* Place on baking sheet: Line a baking sheet with parchment paper and place the balls on it, leaving some space between each.
* Bake: Preheat your oven to 350°F (175°C). Bake the balls for 20-25 minutes, or until they are golden

Dog Friendly Pizza

Ingredients:
* 1 pre-made cauliflower pizza base or other dog friendly base
* 1/4 cup grated cheddar cheese
* 1/4 cup shredded pre-cooked chicken breast
* 1/4 cup grated carrot
* 2-3 finely chopped spinach leaves
* Any dog safe veggies you want to add

Equipment:
* Baking sheet
* Parchment paper

Instructions:
* Preheat your oven to 400°F (200°C).
* Place the pre-made crust on a baking sheet lined with parchment paper.
* Top with grated cheese, chicken, spinach and grated veggies
* Bake for 7-9 minutes, or until the cheese is melted and bubbly.
* Cool, slice and serve to your dog.

Remember: with a pre-made base, it's important to avoid ingredients that are toxic to dogs.
And ensure your dog doesn't consume excessive amounts of cheese.

Mojito Mayhem Cocktail Party Bites

Ingredients:
* 1 cucumber, peeled & thinly sliced into rounds
* 1/4 cup plain, non-fat Greek yogurt (or substitute for cream cheese)
* 1/4 cup mashed carrot
* 1/4 teaspoon dried parsley

Equipment:
* Small bowl
* Spatula or butter knife

Instructions:
* Prepare the cucumber rounds: Slice the cucumber into thin rounds.
* Mix the topping: In a small bowl, combine the plain yogurt, mashed carrot, and dried parsley. Mix well until smooth.
* Assemble the treats: Place a dollop of the yogurt mixture on each cucumber round.
* Serve: Serve the cucumber rounds to your dog as a healthy and refreshing treat.

Tips:
* For a sweeter treat, you can add a small amount of honey or maple syrup to the yogurt mixture

Cocktail Crustini With Salmon

Ingredients:
* 1 loaf of bread, sliced into thin rounds
* Fresh or canned salmon, drained and sliced
* 1/4 cup plain cream cheese

Instructions:
* Toast the bread: Toast the bread slices in toaster or oven to your desired level of crispiness.
* Prepare the salmon: Thinly sliced
* Assemble: Spread cream cheese on crustini, top with sliced salmon

Tip:
Get fancy & sprinkle with dried parsley or dill for a more high end look to your doggy treat plate! Substitute cream cheese with Greek yogurt for a lighter calorie snack.

Any dog safe fish or meat can be thinly sliced & used to top the crustinis for a variety of flavours!

Egg & Chicken Party Mini Quiches

Ingredients:
* 1 cup whole wheat flour
* 1/4 cup water
* 1 egg
* 1/4 cup shredded chicken
* 1/4 cup grated carrot
* 1/4 cup peas

Instructions:
* Preheat oven: Preheat your oven to 350°F (175°C).
* Prepare muffin tin: Line a muffin tin with paper liners.
* Combine wet and dry ingredients: Gradually add the wet ingredients to the dry ingredients, mixing until just combined.
* Divide batter: Divide the batter evenly among the muffin liners.
* Add toppings: Top each muffin with shredded chicken, grated carrot, and peas.
* Bake: Bake for 20-25 minutes, or until the quiches are golden brown and set.
* Cool: Let the quiches cool before serving.

Turkey Meatballs

Ingredients:
* 1 pound ground turkey
* 1/2 cup whole wheat flour
* 1/4 cup plain yogurt
* 1/4 cup grated carrot
* 1/4 cup frozen peas
* 1 egg
* 1/4 teaspoon dried parsley

Instructions:
* Preheat oven: Preheat your oven to 350°F (175°C).
* Combine ingredients: In a large bowl, combine the ground turkey, whole wheat flour, yogurt, carrot, peas, egg, and parsley. Mix well until combined.
* Shape meatballs: Roll the mixture into small meatballs, about 1 inch in diameter.
* Coat in olive oil: Place the meatballs on a baking sheet lined with parchment paper and coat them lightly with olive oil.
* Bake: Bake the meatballs for 20-25 minutes, or until cooked through and browned.
* Cool: Let the meatballs cool slightly before serving.

Tips:
* You can adjust the size of the meatballs to suit your dog's size & preferences.

IPA Bites
Pale Ale Cookies

Ingredients:
* 1/2 cup beef liver, cooked and minced
* 1/4 cup rolled oats
* 1/4 cup whole wheat flour

Instructions:
* Prepare the ingredients: In a mixing bowl, combine the cooked and minced beef liver, rolled oats, and whole wheat flour.
* Mix well: Use a spatula or your hands to thoroughly combine the ingredients until a dough forms.
* Roll into balls: Divide the dough into bite-sized pieces and roll them into balls using your hands or a rolling pin.
* Place on baking sheet: Line a baking sheet with parchment paper and place the balls on it, leaving some space between each.
* Bake: Preheat your oven to 350°F (175°C). Bake the balls for 20-25 minutes, or until they are golden brown.
* Cool completely: Allow the treats to cool completely before giving them to your dog.

Banana & Honey Creamy Dog Ice Cream

Ingredients:
* 1 cup mashed banana
* 1/2 cup plain yogurt
* 1/4 cup plain Greek yogurt
* 1 tablespoon honey

Equipment:
* Blender
* Ice cube tray

Instructions:
* Combine ingredients: Place the mashed banana, plain yogurt, plain Greek yogurt, and honey in a blender.
* Blend until smooth: Blend the ingredients on high speed until the mixture is smooth and creamy.
* Pour into ice cube tray: Pour the mixture into an ice cube tray.
* Freeze: Freeze for at least 2 hours, or until solid.
* Serve: Remove the frozen treats from the ice cube tray and serve to your dog.

Tips:
* Store leftover ice cream treats in an airtight container in the freezer for up to a week

Apple Pie Cookies

Ingredients:
* 1 cup whole wheat flour
* 1/2 cup peanut butter (ensure it doesn't contain xylitol)
* 1/4 cup plain yogurt
* 1/4 cup mashed applesauce
* 1 egg
* 1/4 teaspoon cinnamon

Instructions:
* Preheat oven: Preheat your oven to 350°F (175°C).
* Combine wet ingredients: In a separate bowl, whisk together the peanut butter, yogurt, applesauce, and egg.
* Combine wet and dry ingredients: Gradually add the wet ingredients to the dry ingredients, mixing until just combined.
* Roll out dough: On a lightly floured surface, roll out the dough to about 1/4 inch thickness.
* Cut out shapes: Use dog-shaped cookie cutters or other festive shapes to cut out the dough.
* Place on baking sheet: Place the cut-out cookies on a baking sheet lined with parchment paper.
* Bake: Bake for 10-12 minutes, or until the edges are lightly golden brown.
* Cool: Let the cookies cool completely

Toto's Trifle Cups

Ingredients for layers:
* 1/2 cup peanut butter (ensure it doesn't contain xylitol)
* Pre made cookie crumbles
* 1/4 cup mashed banana
* 1/4 cup plain Greek yogurt
* 1/4 cup blueberries or other fruit

Instructions:
* Prepare the base: Follow the instructions for the dog-friendly apple pie cookies to make a batch of cookies. Cool & crumble for layering.
* Make the banana layer: Combine the mashed banana and plain Greek yogurt in a small bowl.
* Make the blueberry layer: Mash the blueberries.
* Assemble the trifles: Layer the banana mixture, blueberry mixture, peanut butter and crumbled cookie base in the mini bowl or plastic dessert cup in your preferred order to create several thin layers. Top with additional berries, fruit or cookie crumbles.

Turkey Bacon

Ingredients:
* boneless, skinless turkey breast, thinly sliced into strips

Instructions:
* Preheat oven: Preheat your oven to 275°F (135°C).
* Prepare baking sheet: Line a baking sheet with parchment paper.
* Arrange turkey strips: Lay the turkey strips in a single layer on the prepared baking sheet, making sure they don't overlap.
* Bake: Place the baking sheet in the oven and bake for 2-3 hours, or until the turkey strips are completely dried and crispy. The strips should be brittle and break easily when snapped.
* Cool: Remove the baking sheet from the oven and let the turkey strips cool completely on the pan before serving

Tip:
Try different protein like chicken or beef.

Doggy Birthday Cake

Ingredients:
* 1 cup whole wheat flour
* 1/2 cup peanut butter (ensure it doesn't contain xylitol)
* 1/4 cup water
* 1 egg * 1/4 cup mashed banana

Instructions:
* Preheat oven: Preheat your oven to 350°F (175°C).
* Combine dry ingredients: In a mixing bowl, whisk together the whole wheat flour.
* Combine wet ingredients: In a separate bowl, whisk together the peanut butter, water, egg, and banana.
* Combine wet and dry ingredients: Gradually add the wet ingredients to the dry ingredients, mixing until just combined.
* Pour into pan: Pour the batter into a greased and floured cake pan.
* Bake: Bake for 25-30 minutes, or until a toothpick inserted into the center comes out clean.
* Cool: Let the cake cool completely before frosting.

Optional Frosting:
* 1/4 cup plain yogurt
* 1 tablespoon honey * 1/4 teaspoon cinnamon

Combine the yogurt, honey, and cinnamon in a small bowl and mix until smooth. Frost cake!

Gingerbread Cookies

Ingredients:
* 1 cup whole wheat flour
* 1/2 cup peanut butter (ensure it doesn't contain xylitol)
* 1/4 cup water * 1 egg
* 1/4 teaspoon ground ginger

Instructions:
* Preheat oven: Preheat your oven to 350°F (175°C).
* Combine dry ingredients: In a mixing bowl, whisk together the whole wheat flour and ground ginger.
* Combine wet ingredients: In a separate bowl, whisk together the peanut butter, water, and egg.
* Combine wet and dry ingredients: Gradually add the wet ingredients to the dry ingredients, mixing until just combined.
* Roll out dough: On a lightly floured surface, roll out the dough to about 1/4 inch thickness.
* Cut out shapes: Use dog-shaped cookie cutters or other festive shapes to cut out the dough.
* Place on baking sheet: Place the cut-out cookies on a baking sheet lined with parchment paper.
* Bake: Bake for 10-12 minutes, or until the edges are lightly golden brown.
* Cool: Let the cookies cool completely & serve!

Summer Sorbet

Ingredients:
* 1 cup frozen berries (strawberries, blueberries, or a combination)
* 1/2 cup plain yogurt
* 1/4 cup water

Equipment:
* Blender
* Ziploc bag
* Sea salt

Instructions:
* Combine ingredients: Place the frozen berries, yogurt, and water in a blender.
* Blend until smooth: Blend the ingredients on high speed until the mixture is smooth and creamy.
* Pour into bag: Pour the mixture into a Ziploc bag.
* Add salt: Sprinkle a small amount of sea salt on the outside of the bag.
* Mash and freeze: Place the bag in a bowl and mash the mixture for a few minutes. Then, place the bag in the freezer for at least 2 hours, or until solid.
* Serve: Remove the sorbet from the bag and serve to your dog.

Tips:
* For a smoother texture, mash the mixture in the bag every 30 minutes during the freezing process.

Fresh & Healthy Fruits & Vegetables

Slice & dice some fruit or vegetable sticks as a quick & nutritious snack for your pet!
Create a vegetable dip with cream cheese or yogurt!

Fruits:
* Apples (without the core or seeds)
* Bananas
* Blueberries
* Cantaloupe
* Cranberries
* Grapes (seedless)
* Mangoes
* Oranges (peeled)
* Peaches (peeled)
* Pears (peeled)
* Pineapple (peeled)
* Raspberries
* Strawberries
* Watermelon (seedless)

Vegetables:
* Carrots
* Broccoli
* Celery
* Cucumbers
* Green beans
* Peas
* Spinach
* Squash (butternut, acorn, spaghetti)
* Sweet potatoes
* Zucchini
* Asparagus
* Brussels sprouts
* Cauliflower
* Green beans
* Lettuce (romaine, iceberg)

Thank you for purchasing our book!
We hope it becomes an invaluable tool to help you create beautiful memories with your fur baby!

Please consider gifting a copy to your pet parent friends or family members to help us spread the cheer & provide safe & fun resources for dog lovers!

Here's a Cheers to you & your pup!!

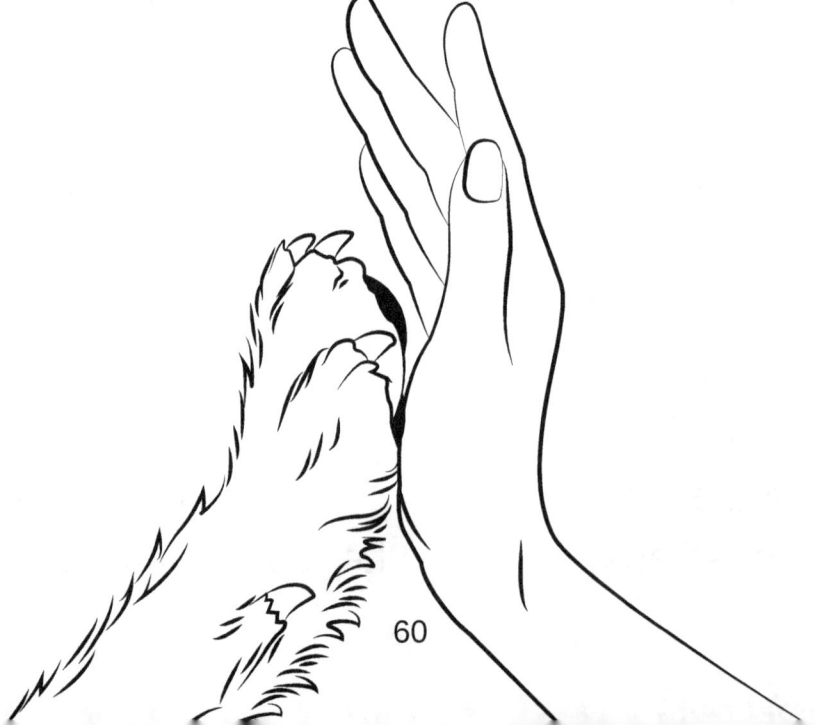

www.ingramcontent.com/pod-product-compliance
Lightning Source LLC
Chambersburg PA
CBHW080325080526
44585CB00021B/2480